James Joyce's The Dead

JAMES JOYCE'S
THE DEAD

A Musical

Based on the Story by
James Joyce

Book by
Richard Nelson

Music by
Shaun Davey

Lyrics Conceived and Adapted by
Richard Nelson and Shaun Davey

GARDEN CITY, NEW YORK

James Joyce's The Dead © 1995 Richard Nelson and Shaun Davey

ISBN: 0-7394-1525-5

James Joyce's THE DEAD premiered at Playwrights Horizons, where it opened on October 28, 1999. The production transferred to Broadway under the auspices of producers Arielle Tepper and Gregory Mosher, where it opened on January 11, 2000. Based on Joyce's short story from his book Dubliners, JAMES JOYCE'S THE DEAD has a book by Richard Nelson, music by Shaun Davey, lyrics adapted and conceived by Mr. Nelson and Mr. Davey and was directed by Mr. Nelson. Sean Curran was the choreographer and Charles Prince the musical director. The production features scenic design by David Jenkins, costumes by Jane Greenwood, lighting by Jennifer Tipton and sound by Scott Lehrer.

THE CAST

Gabriel Conroy	Christopher Walker
Lily	Brooke Sunny Moriber
Mrs. Malins	Paddy Croft
Rita/Young Julia	Daisy Eagan
Michael	Dashiell Eaves
Aunt Julia	Sally Ann Howes
Bartell D'Arcy	John Kelly
Aunt Kate	Marni Nixon
Gretta Conroy	Blair Brown
Mr. Brown	Brian Davies
Miss Molly Ivors	Alice Ripley
Mary Jane	Emily Skinner
Freddy	Stephen Spinella

TIME

Near the turn of the century

PLACE

The Misses Morkans' annual Christmas-time part. Dublin.

Scene One

Drawing Room of the Misses Morkans' home, Dublin. Near the turn of the century.

Piano, a few chairs, sofa, side-table, etc. Family photographs on the piano.

Downstage represents the second floor hallway just outside the drawing room. A violinist and a cellist near the piano.

Gabriel Conroy (forties) enters and speaks to the audience.

GABRIEL: The Misses Morkans' annual Christmas party was always a great musical affair.

(The cellist begins to play the opening instrumental. Aunt Julia, Aunt Kate and Mary Jane enter leading the maid, Lily)

Everybody who knew them came. Members of the family . . . (*gestures to himself*), friends, (*Mr. Browne, Mrs. Malins and Miss Ivors enter. Gabriel gestures to them*) as well as the occasional musical "celebrity" who happened to be visiting Dublin. (*Bartell D'Arcy enters. Gabriel gestures to him*) A student of Aunt Julia's, (*gestures to the violinist*) another of Aunt Kate's, (*gestures to the cellist*), even two of Mary Jane's who were grown up enough . . . (*A boy, Michael, and a girl, Rita, enter. He sits at the piano.*

1

She holds a flute) would be engaged to entertain. Never once did it fall flat. For thirty years there was a party.

(*They all begin to mingle and socialize—music continues, the cellist is joined by others*)

Ever since leaving the house in Stoney Batter, after the death of their brother Pat. The Aunts took with them Pat's daughter, Mary Jane to live here in this dark gaunt house on Usher's Island. The upper part they rent from Mr. Fulham—the cornfactor on the ground floor. He (*three thumps from below*) was never invited.

(*Mary Jane comes around the group greeting them*)

Mary Jane is now the main prop of the household, she has the organ in Haddington Road. She has been through the Academy and gives the pupils' concert each year in the upper room of the Antient Concert Rooms. Many of her pupils belong to the better class families—those on the Kingstown and Dalkey line. But old as they are, the aunts still do their share. (*We see Aunt Kate and Aunt Julia handing out drinks, greeting, smiling, etc.*) Aunt Julia, until quite recently, had been lead soprano at the Church of the Immaculate Conception or—Adam and Eve's as it's generally known. Her retirement was—how should one put it?—not without tears. And Aunt Kate will continue to give lessons here in this room until her dying day.

(*Music stops for a moment. Music starts again*)

An angel passed. The world, I've come to think is like the surface of a frozen lake. We walk along, we slip, we try to keep our balance and not to fall. One day there's a crack, and so we learn that underneath us—is an unimaginable depth. (*Beat*) According to the newspapers that night, snow would be general all over Ireland. For thirty years the Misses Morkans' gave their party. And for thirty years—everyone sang and everyone danced.

(*Gabriel, "the narrator," exits. Music goes into full swing and chatter in the drawing room gets quite loud*)

BROWNE: And may we have some more refreshment? God help me, it's the Doctor's orders.

IVORS: Oh, now, Mr. Browne, I'm sure the doctor never ordered anything of the kind.

BROWNE: Well, you see I'm like the famous Mrs. Cassidy, who is reported to have said: "Now, Mary Grimes, if I don't take it, make me take it, for I feel I want it!"

(*Laughter from the group. Gabriel, "the character," enters the hallway having just arrived. Lily, the maid, and Gretta are behind him. Lily is helping Gretta and Gabriel with their coats and hats*)

LILY: Oh, Mr. Conroy, Miss Kate and Miss Julia thought you were never coming.

GABRIEL: I'll engage they did, but they forgot that

3

my wife here takes three mortal hours to dress herself, and another two just to fix the hair.

LILY: Is it snowing again, Mrs. Conroy?

GRETTA: Yes Lily, I think we are in for a night of it. How's Aunt Julia? We heard she has taken to her bed.

LILY: That was this morning, miss. She was herself again once the music started.

GRETTA: Have they begun the singing yet?

LILY: Not yet miss. But they are talking about it.

(*Aunt Kate and Aunt Julia enter from the drawing room into the hallway. In the drawing room Mary Jane, like a mother hen, checks on and hovers over her two students as the musicians continue the instrumental. The next few lines overlap*)

JULIA: There you are!

KATE (*at the same time*): We were getting worried!

JULIA: Gabriel you look so handsome!

KATE (*over this*): Our favorite nephew!

JULIA: You look lovely too Gretta.

(*Gabriel hands Lily his and his wife's coats*)

KATE: Mary Jane tells us you're not going to take a cab back to Monkstown tonight.

GABRIEL: We had quite enough of that last year, didn't we? (*He turns to Gretta*) Don't you remember, Aunt Kate, what a cold Gretta got out of it? Cab windows rattling all the way, and the east wind blowing in after we passed Marrion. Very jolly it was. Gretta caught a dreadful cold.

JULIA: Quite right, you can't be too careful.

GABRIEL: But as for Gretta, she'd walk home in the snow if she were let.

GRETTA: Oh, but you'll never guess what he makes me wear now!! (*Laughs*) Galoshes! That's the latest. Whenever it's wet underfoot I must put on my galoshes. Tonight even he wanted me to put them on, but I wouldn't. The next thing he'll buy for me will be a diving suit.

(*They all laugh*)

JULIA: And what are galoshes, Gabriel?

KATE: Galoshes, Julia! Goodness me, don't you know what galoshes are? You wear them over your . . . over your boots, Gretta, isn't it?

GRETTA: Yes. Rubbery—guttaperchas things. We both have a pair now. Gabriel says everyone wears them on the continent.

JULIA: Oh, on the continent. (*She nods slowly*)

(*Gretta takes the Aunts' arms and heads for the drawing room*)

GRETTA: Who's here? Are we the last?

KATE: It was only you and Freddy Malins.

(*Gretta sees that Gabriel is not following*)

JULIA: Freddy's mother's here. Poor woman.

GRETTA: Gabriel, you can't hide in the hallway all night.

GABRIEL: I'll be right there.

GRETTA (*to Aunts*): He's terribly anxious about giving his speech. You look so young tonight! No, you do! Both of you!

(*They enter the drawing room—we hear and see the greetings. In the hallway, Gabriel takes a piece of paper out of his pocket—his speech—and glances at it. Lily returns for the rest of the gloves, scarves, etc.*)

GABRIEL: Tell me, Lily, do you still go to school?

LILY: Oh no, sir. I'm done schooling this year and more.

GABRIEL: Oh, then, I suppose we'll be going to your

wedding one of these fine days, with your young man, eh?

LILY: The men that is now is only all palaver and what they can get out of you. (*She turns to leave*)

GABRIEL: Oh Lily—it's Christmas time, isn't it? (*He tries to hand her a coin*)

LILY: Oh no, sir! Really, sir, I wouldn't take it.

GABRIEL (*pushing the coin into her hand*): Christmas time! Christmas time!

LILY: Well—thank you, sir.

GABRIEL: Health and good cheer.

(*Lily exits back down the hallway. In the drawing room, the music ends. Applause. In the hallway, Gabriel has taken out the speech again. Miss Ivors comes out of the drawing room, looking for Gabriel*)

IVORS: So there you are! I saw Gretta and knew you must be in tow.

GABRIEL: I'm not in tow.

IVORS: Is that your speech? I heard you're making the speech.

GABRIEL: It's not a speech, Molly, it's a toast—

IVORS: I'm sorry I shall miss it. I'm not staying for dinner.

GABRIEL: You're not staying—?

IVORS: No. I can't. (*Beat*) I have a crow to pluck with you, Mr. Conroy.

GABRIEL: With me?

IVORS: Yes. Who is G.C.?

GABRIEL: What do you mean?

IVORS: Oh, innocent Amy! I have found out you are the G.C. writing for the *Daily Express*. Now, aren't you ashamed of yourself? Writing for a rag like that.

GABRIEL: I write book reviews—

IVORS: I didn't think, Gabriel Conroy, that you were a West Briton.

GABRIEL: I am not a West Briton!!

(*This shout quiets the drawing room for an instant. There Browne has brought Bartell D'Arcy to Gretta to introduce him. We hear from the drawing room*):

BROWNE: I'm trying to get Mr. Bartell D'Arcy to sing later on. All Dublin is raving about him.

KATE: Shouldn't we begin the singing, Gabriel and Gretta have arrived so we're mostly here?

MALINS: My son isn't here.

MARY JANE: He'll be here, Mrs. Malins.

MALINS: And he'll be screwed.

(In the drawing room, Mary Jane begins to organize the musicians for the next song. Lily has come back down the hallway and into the drawing room. She goes to the Aunts for instructions. In the hallway):

IVORS: If you're not a West Briton perhaps you'd like to join us on an excursion this summer to the Aran Islands?

GABRIEL: The Aran Islands?

IVORS: Gretta's from Connaught, isn't she?

GABRIEL: Her people are.

IVORS: It would be splendid, Mr. Conroy.

GABRIEL: I have already arranged to go—

IVORS: Where?

GABRIEL: Every year I go for a cycling tour with some fellows and so—

IVORS: Yes, but where?

GABRIEL: Well, we go to France or Belgium or perhaps Germany.

IVORS: And why go to France and Belgium and Germany instead of visiting your own land?

GABRIEL: It's partly to keep in touch with the languages and partly for a change.

(*In the drawing room we hear*):

KATE: Mary Jane's been practicing us to our death.

(*In the hallway*):

GABRIEL: I think they are going to start the singing—

IVORS: And haven't your own language to keep in touch with—Irish?

GABRIEL: If it comes to that, you know, Irish is not my language.

IVORS: And haven't you your own land to visit, that you know nothing of, your own people, your own country?!

(*The argument has drawn the attention of the drawing room. Mary Jane tries to get the singing started*)

GABRIEL: To tell you the truth I'm sick of my own country!!!

(*Pause. Everyone heard this*)

MARY JANE: This is a lovely tune that I heard for the first time just last week—

(*Gabriel goes into the drawing room*)

GABRIEL (*to Gretta*): I thought the singing was to start. Where is the singing?

MARY JANE (*to Gabriel, explaining*): Yes. That's right, yes it is. This is a lovely tune I heard for the first time just last week . . .

(*Ivors goes into the drawing room*)

IVORS (*to Gabriel*): West Briton!!

MARY JANE: This is a lovely tune I heard for the first time just last week based upon the words by the poet Michael William Balfe, I believe . . . (*Gathers Kate and Rita*) Ladies and Gentlemen?

MARY JANE, AUNT KATE & RITA (*singing*):
By Killarney's lakes and fells,
Em'rald isles and winding bays,
Mountain paths, and woodland dells;

Mem'ry ever fondly strays,
Bounteous nature loves all lands,
Beauty wanders ev'ry where;

(*Gretta puts her arm around Gabriel, and offers him a sip from her drink.*

During the song, Mrs. Malins suddenly stands, worried about her son, and goes into the hallway to wait. Others are concerned but say nothing. In the hallway she tries not to cry)

Footprints leaves on many strands,
But her home is surely there,
Angels fold their wings and rest!

In that Eden of the West,
Beauty's home, Killarney
Ever fair, Killarney.

(They bow. Polite applause. Gabriel goes back into the hallway, Gretta follows, Mrs. Malins is now there)

GRETTA: What words had you with Molly Ivors?

GABRIEL: No words.

(Beat)

GRETTA: We are trying to get that Mr. D'Arcy to sing. He's full of conceit, I think.

GABRIEL: There were no words, she wanted us to go for a trip to the west of Ireland and I said I wouldn't.

GRETTA: Oh, let's go, Gabriel. I'd love to see Galway again.

GABRIEL: You can go if you like.

GRETTA (*turns to Mrs. Malins*): That's a nice husband for you Mrs. Malins. (*Beat*) He'll be here, Mrs. Malins.

(*Music ends in the drawing room. Polite applause*)

GABRIEL: Why do I let someone like Molly Ivors bother me so?

GRETTA: I don't know Gabriel.

GABRIEL: She is so—what's the word? Confident. It's her confidence that's . . . How can she be so damn sure she is right?

GRETTA: She's young?

GABRIEL: When I was young I respected my elders. I didn't make fun of them.

GRETTA: And she's just teasing you. So, tease her back, Gabriel. (*Gabriel goes back into drawing room. Gretta turns back to Mrs. Malins*) He'll be here any minute, Mrs. Malins.

(*Gretta follows Gabriel back into the drawing room*)

MARY JANE (*pulling Michael out from behind the piano*): Now Michael here. Is in truth from the Killarney Lakes! And a fine student as well. Don't go blushing now, Michael. (*To Gretta as she enters*) Is Gabriel all right? We heard voices in the hall.

GRETTA: It wasn't a thing, Mary Jane. Not a thing.

MARY JANE (*to everyone*): We're getting hungry and when we're hungry we are quarrelsome.

D'ARCY: And when we are thirsty we are also quarrelsome.

GRETTA: And when we have quenched that thirst— we are sometimes also quarrelsome too.

MARY JANE: This is true. (*To Michael*) So tell us what are you going to sing? (*Then without letting him answer*) No, rather—shall it be a surprise? But let it be said that it was Michael's own idea. And he thought it might be especially poignant after what's just been sung.

MICHAEL (*to the musicians*): Now I once knew a girl like this. (*Michael begins to sing to the others whose minds are on other things*)

O did you ever hear of Kate
Wait till I tell you, wait till I tell you
She'll get you in a terrible state
Should you visit the banks of Killarney.

Gentlemen, beware the smile
For many's the wile lies hid in the smile
Of lovely Kate, just you wait
Till you visit the banks of Killarney.

(*Mary Jane joins, trying to get the others involved*)

MARY JANE AND MICHAEL:
That eye so modestly beaming
You'd never think of the mischief
She's dreaming—fatal's the spell
That lurks in the eye of Kate Kearney.

BROWNE (*to Miss Ivors, a little too loud, so others*
hear): That sounds like Molly Ivors.

(*Lily enters quickly from the hallway*)

MICHAEL:
Just one look is all it took
Wait til I tell you.

MARY JANE:
Wait till I tell you.

MICHAEL:
So if you chance to stray
You'll likely stay on the banks of Killarney.

(*Lily whispers to Kate first, then to Julia*)

MICHAEL:
Don't mistake the charms of Kate
Wait till I tell you.

MARY JANE AND COMPANY (*with Mary Jane con-*
ducting the others):
Wait till I tell you.

MICHAEL:
Discretion is the best escape
So shun the dangers and fly.

(*Julia approaches Gabriel, whispers to him. Gabriel leaves the room, goes down the hallway and exits, passing a concerned Mrs. Malins*)

MICHAEL, MARY JANE AND COMPANY:
That eye so modestly beaming
You'd never think of the mischief
She's dreaming—fatal's the spell
That lurks in the eye of Kate Kearney.

She lives on the Banks of Killarney
From the glance of her eye
Shun the dangers and fly
For fatal's the glance of Kate Kearney.

MICHAEL:
Should you ever meet this Kate
Wait till I tell you.

COMPANY:
Wait till I tell you.

(*From off we hear Freddy, shouting, then singing, and Gabriel shushing*)

MICHAEL:
Don't go to the same sad fate
As many who visit Killarney.

Though she looks so sweet and simple

COMPANY:
  Trouble lies in every dimple.

MICHAEL:
  Who inhales her spicy gale
  Dies by the breath of Kate Kearney.

COMPANY:
  That eye so modestly beaming
  You'd never think of the mischief
  She's dreaming—fatal's the spell
  That lurks in the eye of Kate Kearney.

  She lives on the banks of Killarney
  From the glance of her eye
  Shun the dangers and fly for
  Fatal's the glance of Kate Kearney.

  That eye so modestly beaming
  You'd never think of the mischief
  She's dreaming—fatal's the spell
  That lurks in the eye of Kate Kearney.

(*End of song. From off we hear a drunken Freddy singing*)

FREDDY (*off*):
  That eye so modestly beaming
  You'd never think of the mischief
  She's dreaming . . .

(*The Aunts hurry into the hallway*)

MALINS (*nearly in tears, to the Aunts*): He's screwed. I knew he'd be screwed. Don't let him in if he's screwed!

(*Mrs. Malins hurries into the drawing room. Gabriel comes down the hallway*)

KATE (*to Gabriel*): He's not so bad, is he?

GABRIEL: Oh, no. Hardly noticeable.

(*Gabriel goes back into drawing room. Freddy comes down the hallway singing and happy*)

FREDDY: I heard the glorious singing from the street, and like a beacon it was—(*sees the cold look in the Aunts' eyes*) Julia, Kate . . . I suppose my mother's here?

JULIA: She's sitting right in there, Freddy.

FREDDY: Has she—been here long?

(*They don't answer. They go into the drawing room. He hesitates, then follows*)

IVORS (*greeting*): Good evening, Freddy.

GRETTA: Hello, Freddy.

JULIA: Won't you sit down, Freddy?

GRETTA (*stands to give him her seat next to his mother*): Oh yes, here Freddy, come.

(*Freddy sees his mother for the first time and heads for the sofa*)

BROWNE: Now, then, Teddy. We're going to fill you out a good glass of lemonade just to buck you up.

FREDDY: I apologize if I'm . . . late.

KATE: And his poor mother made him take the pledge. She's been telling everyone.

(*Others shush her, then quiet. No one knows what to say or do, then*):

FREDDY: I just heard a story . . . on my way here . . .

GRETTA (*changing the subject*): Are you with us long Mrs. Malins? You're a joy to see.

MALINS: I leave on Tuesday.

GRETTA: I hear Scotland is a beautiful place.

MALINS: My daughter takes fine care of me. Bless her. And her husband too.

GRETTA: Isn't that grand.

(*Pause. No one knows what to say*)

MALINS: What a splendid man he is, my son-in-law. And an excellent fisherman too. One day he caught us a fish, a big fish, and he gave it to the man at the local hotel to boil for our dinner.

GRETTA: Well isn't that grand.

(*Again, what to say? Then*):

KATE: Mary Jane?

MARY JANE (*new idea*): Michael?

GRETTA: Yes, another song by Michael.

MARY JANE: Yes. I think some of you may know this . . .

GABRIEL: Which—?

KATE (*at the same time*): What's he going to—?

MARY JANE: The Parnell song.

(*Everyone starts shouting at once: they hate this song, they love it, others just know it will cause trouble*)

JULIA: Oh not that song!

KATE (*same time*): Please, Mary Jane.

MARY JANE (*same time*): It's a lovely song.

GABRIEL: Aren't we tired of simplistic patriotism? I hate this song. It's mindless.

IVORS: I love it.

GABRIEL (*to Molly*): Do you now? What a surprise!

(*Michael, drum in hand, begins "Parnell's Plight," with Rita on the accordion*)

MICHAEL (*sings*):
Who fears to speak of Parnell's plight?

(*Molly suddenly joins in. Others react*)

MICHAEL & IVORS:
Who blushes at the name?
When cowards mock our patriot's fight
Who hangs his head in shame?
Who hangs his head in shame?

(*Michael lets her have the song*)

IVORS:
He's all a knave and half a slave
Who slights his country thus
But a true man
Like you man
Will fill your glass with us!
Will fill your glass with us!

FREDDY (*to Michael*): She pinched your song!

IVORS:
Some on the shores of distant lands
Their weary hearts have laid
And by the strangers heedless hands
Their lonely graves were made

21

(*D'Arcy asks to play Rita's accordion, and does so for the rest of the song*)

IVORS & MICHAEL:
Their lonely graves were made.

IVORS:
But though their clay be far away
Beyond the Atlantic foam
To you men, I say men—

(*Gabriel suddenly jumps in, topping Ivors*):

GABRIEL:
For Christ sake don't come home!

(*Laughter at this interruption and deflating of this song. These "other" lyrics have gone around the Dublin pubs, etc.*)

GRETTA: Gabriel!

BROWNE AND GABRIEL:
For Christ sake don't come home!

(*Michael and Freddy join them*)

MEN:
We owe our duty to Ireland and
We hold her honor in our hand.

(*They hold up their drinks—the honor they hold in their hands. Laughter*)

Through low and high land
Come all free men make a stand.

(*Molly takes the floor*)

IVORS:
They rose in dark and evil days
To right their native soil.

GABRIEL:
They rose in dark and evil ways
And avoided work and toil.

GABRIEL & MEN:
And avoided work and toil!

(*More laughter, Miss Ivors just stares at him for a moment. This is now a battle between Gabriel and Miss Ivors—the continuation of their argument in the hallway*)

GABRIEL (*making fun of her*):
Let's drink the memory of the brave
And the one or two who stay—

IVORS (*grabbing Gabriel*):
To you men,
True men who—
Are not getting away!

(*The women laugh at this, the room is warming up*)

IVORS, LILY AND RITA:
Who are not getting away!

BOTH GROUPS:
　　We owe our duty to Ireland and
　　We hold her honor in our hand.

　　Through low and high land
　　Come all freemen make a stand.

MICHAEL & IVORS:
　　Off to the shores of distant lands
　　Their weary hearts they bear.
　　To work all day with calloused hand
　　For a wage both good and fair.

BOTH GROUPS:
　　For a wage both good and fair.

(*Gretta suddenly takes the floor*)

GRETTA:
　　With wives abandoned like the mist
　　With babies left forgot
　　To you men
　　To you I speak
　　Watch out before you rot.

GRETTA, KATE, JULIA AND MRS. MALINS:
　　Watch out before you rot!

(*All sing, sway, clap, laugh and dance*)

ALL:
　　We owe our duty to Ireland
　　We hold her honor in our hand

**Through low and high land
Come all freemen make a stand**

**We owe our duty to Ireland
We hold her honor in our hand
Through low and high land
Come all freemen make a stand**

**We owe our duty to Ireland
We hold her honor in our hand
Through low and high land
Come all freemen make a stand**

MICHAEL: One more time then!

ALL:
**We owe our duty to Ireland
We hold her honor in our hand
Through low and high land
Come all freemen make a stand.**

(*The song ends, but it is not over yet as the violinist suddenly begins playing a jig*)

IVORS: Six hand jig!

(*And the song has turned into a dance. Partners are picked. Soon they must all dance, changing partners down a line, etc.*)

(*Freddy, during this, crosses between dancers and goes across the room to his mother. He gets on his knees, and finally she relents and takes his hand and the two begin to dance together. Mother has now forgiven son*)

(*At one point in the song, Gretta and the young Michael find themselves dancing—facing each other: Gretta is oddly affected by Michael*)

(*All dance. And the party has finally begun! As they finish, a flushed Molly Ivors*):

IVORS: I'm staying for dinner, now!

GRETTA: You're the comical girl, Molly Ivors. (*Bangs from downstairs—Mr. Fulham*) Oh, Mr. Fulham!

(*The banging stops, and the party has quieted a bit*)

MARY JANE: Who wants to sing next?

(*All have suggestions, then*):

MICHAEL: How about Mr. and Mrs. Conroy!?

(*Others agree*)

GABRIEL: I'm sure someone else must wish to . . .

(*A hesitant Gabriel is pushed toward the piano*)

MARY JANE: What do you want to sing Gabriel?

GABRIEL: It's the same from last year.

GRETTA: We haven't had the time—what with the children. Oh dear, Gabriel. We should have rehearsed more.

(They sit, and Gabriel begins to sing "Adieu to Bally-shannon" to the others)

GABRIEL:
  Adieu to Ballyshannon
  Where I was bred and born.
  Go where I may, I'll think of you,
  As sure as night and morn
  I'll leave my warm heart with you
  Although my back I'm forced to turn—
  And so adieu to Ballyshannon,
  And the winding banks of Erne.

GRETTA:
  There's not a house or window,
  There's not a field or hill,
  But, east or west, in foreign lands
  They recollect them still.
  My loving friends I'll bear in mind
  And often shall I fondly turn
  To think of lovely Ballyshannon
  And the winding banks of Erne.

GABRIEL:
  The music of the waterfall,
  The mirror of the tide,
  When all the green-hilled harbor
  Is full from side to side—
  A thousand chances are to one
  That I never may return
  And so adieu to Ballyshannon,
  And the winding banks of Erne.

BOTH:
> Adieu to evening dances,
> Where merry neighbors meet
> And the fiddle says to boys and girls
> "Get up and shake your feet!"
> The mournful song of exile now
> Is all that's left for me to learn
> And so adieu my dear companions
> And the winding banks of Erne,
> And so adieu my dear companions
> And the winding banks of Erne.

(*Michael sits at the piano and plays as Gabriel and Gretta stand and dance a waltz for the others, who are moved. As they finish, others applaud*)

GRETTA: I think we sang it better last year.

MALINS: And we shall make you sing it every year. It cannot be heard enough.

MICHAEL: It's a lovely tune.

BROWNE (*standing, presenting Julia*): Now, my latest discovery! Miss Julia Morkan!

(*A hesitant Julia stands*)

FREDDY: Well Browne, if you are serious you might make a worse discovery.

BROWNE: I'm serious.

SCENE ONE

(*Kate takes her place at the piano, she will accompany her sister*)

FREDDY: All I can say is, I love Julia's voice. And I have been coming here for—how many years? And every year I love her voice. It gets better every year—

BROWNE: I agree!

FREDDY: I swear it does. That is the honest truth. Her voice improves with time. How many times have I told you, Julia Morkan, you are thrown away in that choir, with such a voice. (*Others try to shush him*) That choir is so fortunate to have you among it. If I were that choir director . . . (*Finally notices the others trying to get him to stop*) What? What? What am I sayin', but the God's truth?

(*Awkward pause*)

MARY JANE: Aunt Julia has retired from the choir, Freddy. Haven't you heard that?

FREDDY (*confused*): Retired?? But that's impossible!

KATE (*it comes out*): Yes, after years of slaving there night and day, night and day. Six o'clock on Christmas morning. She was there.

MARY JANE: Yes but wasn't it for the honor of God, Aunt Kate?

29

KATE: I know all about the honor of God, Mary Jane, but I don't think it is at all honorable to turn women out of choirs who have slaved there all their lives and put those little whipper-snappers in their place. It's not right. Is what I think. It's not just.

(*Awkward pause*)

FREDDY: Well then—we are the more fortunate to have Julia Morkan sing but for us.

JULIA: I don't have much of a voice anymore. You all know that. But I'll sing if you insist.

FREDDY: I insist!

(*Julia almost begins, then one more apology*):

JULIA: I did have a nice voice when I was young.

(*Others tell her to stop, and she sings "When Lovely Lady" in a weak voice, which had once been beautiful*):

When lovely lady stoops to folly
And finds too late that men betray
What charms can soothe her melancholy,
What art can wash her grief away?

The only art her guilt to cover
To hide her shame from every eye,
To give repentance to her lover,
And wring his bosom, is—to die.

SCENE ONE

(The singer and the song touch everyone in the room. For a moment, Julia is confused and cannot continue, then Kate begins singing to help her sister)

KATE:
When lovely lady stoops to folly

JULIA AND KATE:
And finds too late that men betray
What charms can soothe her melancholy,
What art can wash her grief away?

(Pause. Others, seeing the frailty of Julia, try not to cry)

JULIA: As I said, I used to have a nice voice.

(Others try to dissuade her, but without conviction)

MARY JANE *(trying to get a hold of herself)*: So um, who wants to sing next? Anybody want to sing next?

BROWNE: Teddy! Teddy always prepares something.

MARY JANE: Have you something, Freddy?

(Browne whispers an idea to Freddy, who laughs, and stands to sing)

MALINS: Don't embarrass me.

FREDDY *(suddenly turns to Julia)*: That was so— lovely, Julia. It really was. *(Browne starts to play the piano. Freddy turns to the others)* It's called "The Three Jolly Pigeons."

MALINS: What does that mean?

GRETTA: It's the name of a pub.

MALINS: Oh God.

FREDDY (*sings and dances, as if in a pub*):
　Let schoolmasters puzzle
　Their brains with grammar
　And nonsense and learning
　I stoutly maintain

　Good liquor gives genius
　A better discerning.
　Folderol-dee, folderol-da

FREDDY & BROWNE:
　Fold-di-dee, fold-di-da
　Fold-di-dee, fold-di-do
　Dee, fold-di-da, fold-di-dee, fold-di-do!

FREDDY:
　When Methodist preachers
　Come into town

GRETTA: Looking for you, Browne!

FREDDY:
　Famed for their preaching
　That drinking is sinful
　I'll wager the rascals
　A hatful of crowns
　That they always preach best with a skinful,

FREDDY AND BROWNE:
  Fold-di-dee, fold-di-da
  Fold-di-dee, fold-di-do
  Dee, fold-di-da, fold-di-dee, fold-di-do!

FREDDY:
  Now come let us put
  The jorum about
  Decorum go hang
  Let's be merry and clever
  Our hearts and our liquors
  Are stout as a tree.

FREDDY AND LILY:
  Here's to the three jolly pigeons forever!

(*Others are surprised that young Lily should know this pub song*)

FREDDY, BROWNE AND OTHERS:
  Fold-di-dee, fold-di-da
  Fold-di-dee, fold-di-do
  Dee, fold-di-da, fold-di-dee, fold-di-do!

FREDDY: Sing, sing, sing!!

EVERYONE:
  Fold-di-dee, fold-di-da
  Fold-di-dee, fold-di-do
  Dee, fold-di-da, fold-di-dee, fold-di-do!

(*They end laughing, except Mrs. Malins, who stands and takes a chagrined Freddy back to his seat*)

MARY JANE: Well Mr. D'Arcy, will you do us the honor now?

(*Others try to get D'Arcy to sing, when Gretta surprises herself and volunteers*)

GRETTA: I have something! (*Beat*) Or should I let someone else—Mr. Browne?

BROWNE: No please, please.

GABRIEL (*surprised*): You prepared something by yourself?

GRETTA: Well no, I didn't know—

GABRIEL: She didn't say a word about preparing something just for herself.

GRETTA: I hadn't. I just . . .

GABRIEL: Just what?

IVORS: Let her sing, Gabriel—

GABRIEL: I wasn't saying she shouldn't—

GRETTA: I remembered a song I used to sing is all. I hadn't even thought about it for years.

KATE (*pointing to the musicians*): Will they know it?

GRETTA: Oh I don't need anyone to play with me. It

comes from the West. (*To Michael, who has begun picking up glasses, etc.*) Ah, but he might know it. Perhaps they sing it in Killarney too?

(*Michael and everyone is confused*)

GABRIEL: Which song is it?

GRETTA (*she closes her eyes to sing*): You don't know it I'm sure. I'm nervous all of a sudden (*Laughs. Mary Jane goes to Michael, whispers to him, he turns to leave*) I hope I can remember . . . (*She opens her eyes and sees Michael leaving*) Why is that young man leaving?

MARY JANE (*confused*): I asked him to check with Lily about the dinner . . .

GRETTA: Should I wait until, he comes back?

KATE: He's not one of the guests, Gretta.

GRETTA: Of course, I'm—well, all right then. Let me see, if I can remember . . .

(*See closes her eyes, others watch her, and Gabriel steps forward and speaks to audience*)

GABRIEL: And then she sang. A song I'd never heard. In a voice, I'd never known.

GRETTA (*sings*)
Lean out of the window

Goldenhair
I heard you singing
A merry air.

My book was closed
I read no more
Watching the fire dancing
On the floor.

I left my book
I left my room
I heard you singing
Through the gloom.
Singing and singing
A merry air
Lean out of the window
Goldenhair.

Arise my beautiful one
Arise, arise.

Arise my beautiful one
Arise, arise.

The night dew lies
Upon my lips and eyes.

The night dew lies
Upon my lips and eyes.

GABRIEL: A song I'd never heard her sing. In a voice
I'd never known. When she'd finished I noticed her
face flush a bright red and her hands tremble. And

she sighed—like a girl. That's what I remember thinking—like a girl. And I was so pleased to be her boy.

GABRIEL (*sings*):
Arise, my beautiful one
Arise, arise.

GRETTA:
Arise, my beautiful one
Arise, Arise.

GRETTA AND GABRIEL:
The new dew lies
Upon my/your lips and eyes.
The night dew lies
Upon my/your lips and eyes.

(*The lights dim as others applaud lightly and praise Gretta's song. Gabriel speaks to us*)

GABRIEL: The Misses Morkans' party continued that year. Other songs were sung, others danced as we waited for dinner. But all I remember—is my wife. My children's mother appearing to me again as the girl of our youth. Gretta—as if pulled back through the dull existence that is time, and back toward the lost moments that are ecstasy. How I desired her. My soul's tender fire was heartier than I'd feared. Children, writing, household cares had not smothered the coals. What was it about her, as she sang that song? She was right, I hadn't known it, though I shall never forget it now. Nor shall I forget that love in her eyes. And the need. It simply did not occur to me at the time, that it wasn't for me.

(*In the dim light, we and Gabriel see Gretta looking at the young Michael*)

(*Suddenly Gabriel turns back to us and sets the next scene, as around and behind him the actors set the tables, etc.*)

The dinner tables that Christmas as with all Christmases past were laden with the care of a general preparing for battle: there lay a great ham, there the goose. And between these rival ends ran parallel lines of side-dishes: two little ministers of jelly, red and yellow; a shallow dish of red jam, Smyrna figs, custard dish, chocolate bowl. And in the center stood, as sentries, two squat old-fashioned decanters of cut glass, one for port, the other sherry. And upon the closed piano, three squadrons of bottles: stout, ale, minerals, ordered according to the colors of their uniforms. Or so it all had looked at the beginning of the siege and before the attack.

(*The table is set for the end of the meal. All are seated and frozen, except for Gabriel*)

I, of course, carved the bird. Took my place at the table. Where at last the smell of the goose, then that of the pudding, and the ever-rising talk and conviviality returned my mind back to this world.

(*As he sits, the table comes to life*)

Scene Two

The Dining Room.

The family and guests—Aunt Kate & Julia, Mary Jane, Gabriel, Gretta, Freddy, Mrs. Malins, Miss Ivors, Browne, and D'Arcy—around a large table, toward the end of the meal. Gabriel sits at one head, the Aunts and Mary Jane are at the other. Lily, Michael and Rita come and go, clearing. There are numerous conversations going on, but one we hear first is:

D'ARCY: The leading contralto though was first rate, wouldn't you say?

FREDDY: Where's this?

BROWNE: The Theatre Royal.

IVORS: I thought she had a rather vulgar style of production.

D'ARCY: Is that what you thought?

FREDDY: Has anyone been to the new pantomime at the Gaiety?

(No one says anything. Of course they haven't, or wouldn't admit it if they had)

D'ARCY: No, Freddy, I don't think any of us have.

FREDDY: Because, now I'd be curious to hear your opinion. I think it's a grand show.

BROWNE: It takes Teddy to find out the really good things.

FREDDY: And why couldn't it be grand? Because it's at the Gaiety? There's a negro chieftain leading every chorus in the panto. (*Freddy crunches celery*)

MALINS: SSShh.

FREDDY: He has one of the finest tenor voices I ever heard on any man. (*Freddy crunches on his celery*)

MALINS: SSShh.

FREDDY (*to his mother*): Celery they say is a capital thing for the blood, Mother.

KATE (*new topic*): Of course you've seen about the room, Gretta.

GRETTA: Oh, the room is all right. We've taken one at the Gresham.

MALINS: The Gresham.

KATE: To be sure, by far the best thing to do.

IVORS: That'll be nice for the two of you.

(*Lily clatters a dish*)

KATE: Lily! SShhh!

IVORS: A night without the children.

KATE: And the children? You're not anxious about them, Gretta?

GRETTA: Oh, for one night. Besides, Bessie will look after them.

KATE: To be sure. What a comfort it is to have a girl like that, one you can depend on.

(*A quick glance at the clumsy Lily, and she hurries back to the kitchen with plates*)

MARY JANE: One of my pupils gave me a pass to *Mignon*. Of course it was very fine, but it did make me think of poor Georgina Burns.

FREDDY: Who's—?

D'ARCY: Oh Freddy, she was a singer. Long ago. Magnificent.

BROWNE: Just to hear that name: Georgina Burns! And a world comes rushing back. The great Trebilli. Giulini.

IVORS: Who?

BROWNE: You don't remember Giulini? Julia remembers him.

JULIA: Mmmmmmmmmmm.

BROWNE: Those were the days—when there was something like singing to be heard in Dublin.

FREDDY (*to the others*): He should go to the Gaiety.

MALINS: Sh-sh.

BROWNE: The top gallery of the old Royal would be packed night after night. One night—an Italian tenor sang five encores to "Let me Like a Soldier Fall," and introduced a high C every time. The gallery boys in their enthusiasm would unyoke the horses from the carriage of the great prima donna and pull her themselves through the streets.

GRETTA (*to Michael, as he passes by her, picking up dishes*): You're not from Galway, by any chance?

MICHAEL: No. Killarney.

GRETTA: Oh that's right. Mary Jane said. No, you reminded me of someone.

BROWNE: Why do they never play the grand old operas, anymore *Dinorah? Lucrezia Borgia?* Perhaps it's because—there aren't the voices to sing them.

D'ARCY: I presume there are as good singers today as there were then.

(*Silence*)

BROWNE: Where are they?

D'ARCY: In London, Paris, Milan. I suppose that Caruso, for example, is quite as good, if not better than any of the men you have mentioned.

BROWNE: Oh maybe so, but I doubt it—Caruso??

MARY JANE: I'd give anything to hear Caruso sing.

KATE: For me—there is only one tenor. To please me, I mean.

BROWNE: And you are notoriously hard to please.

KATE: But I suppose none of you ever heard of him.

D'ARCY: Who was he, Mrs. Morkan?

(*Michael, Lily, Rita exit with most of the plates*)

KATE: His name . . . was Parkinson. I heard him when he was in his prime and I think he had the purest tenor voice that was ever put into a man's throat.

D'ARCY: Strange, I never even heard of him.

BROWNE: Yes, Kate is right. I do remember hearing of old Parkinson. But he's too far back for me.

(*Laughter*)

KATE: Is he? A beautiful pure sweet mellow English tenor. Was he not? Ohh, how I loved that voice.

(*Awkward pause. The sense around the table that her passion was for more than his voice, then to change the subject*):

GRETTA: Gabriel, perhaps this . . .

GABRIEL: Yes, if you like.

(*Julia stands and starts to pick up dishes*)

MARY JANE (*to Julia*): Sit down. Sit—. Lily's here for that. And tonight she's even got help. You know you're not to clean up.

FREDDY (*to his Mother*): I wish you'd smile. (*To the others*) She has a lovely smile. When she smiles.

GABRIEL (*standing, trying to get their attention, tapping a glass*): Excuse me.

KATE: Mr. Browne, you didn't eat your pudding.

MARY JANE: Perhaps it wasn't brown enough.

BROWNE: It was brown, though not as brown as I am. I'm brown all over!

(*Laughter at the terrible pun*)

GABRIEL (*no one is paying attention to him*): Ladies and Gentlemen. (*Taps a glass*) It has fallen to my lot this evening, as in years past, to perform a very pleasing task but a task for which I am afraid my poor powers as a speaker are all too inadequate.

BROWNE: Oh, no!

GABRIEL: But, however that may be, I can only ask you tonight to take the will for the deed and to lend me your attention for a few moments while I endeavor to express in words what my feelings are on this occasion.

(*Julia suddenly drops her glass*)

KATE: Julia?

GRETTA: What?

FREDDY (*explaining*): Julia dropped her glass.

KATE: Julia? Are you all right?

JULIA (*standing*): I just need a little air. That's all. (*Beat*) I won't be long. Just a little air.

(*Julia exits. Mary Jane and Kate suddenly stand and follow her out. Pause. No one knows what to do. Browne pours himself and Freddy a drink*)

FREDDY: No, no, Browne!

BROWNE: For the toast.

(*Freddy turns to his mother, who hesitates, then nods. Pause*)

IVORS: She looked pale all of a sudden.

(*Lily, Rita, Michael enter to clear*)

GRETTA: Did the glass break? (*D'Arcy holds up the unbroken glass*) She looked tired all night.

GABRIEL (*still standing, his speech interrupted*): Maybe I should go and help.

GRETTA: No, they'll get you if they need you, Gabriel. Why don't you sit down?

(*Pause*)

IVORS: Is it still snowing, does anyone know?

LILY: It still is, Miss.

MALINS: My son is going down to Mount Melleray in a week or so.

FREDDY (*explaining*): The monastery.

MALINS: The air is so bracing down there. And the monks are so hospitable. They never ask for a penny from their guests.

BROWNE: Do you mean that a chap can go down there and put up there as if it were a hotel and live on the fat of the land and then come away without paying a farthing?

RITA: Oh, most people give some donation to the monastery as they leave.

BROWNE: I wish we had an institution like that in the Protestant Church.

MALINS: The monks of course, never speak. They get up at two in the morning after sleeping in their coffins.

BROWNE: Why do they sleep in their coffins?

GABRIEL: It's the rule of the order.

BROWNE: Yes, but why?

MALINS: It's a rule.

FREDDY: The monks, you see, are trying to make up for the sins committed by all the sinners in the outside world.

BROWNE: I like that idea, but wouldn't a comfortable spring bed do them as well?

MALINS: The coffin is to remind them of their last end.

GABRIEL: I think I should go and help them.

MALINS: They are very good men, the monks. Very pious men.

IVORS: Here they come Gabriel . . .

(*The women have reentered. Lily, Rita, and Michael exit*)

JULIA: Forgive me Gabriel. Forgive me. It must have been the heat of the kitchen . . .

(*The ladies sit, and turn their attention to Gabriel*)

KATE: Gabriel? You were saying?

GABRIEL (*he hesitates, then*): Ladies and Gentlemen. It is not the first time that we have gathered together under this roof, around this board. It is not the first time that we have been recipients—or perhaps, I had better say, the victims—of the hospitality of certain good ladies.

(*Laughter at the joke*)

I feel more strongly with each recurring year that our country has no tradition which does it so much honor and which it should guard so jealously as that of its hospitality. It is a tradition that is unique as far as my experience goes among modern nations. And I have visited not a few places abroad.

Some might say, perhaps, that with us Irish it is rather a failing than anything to be boasted of. But if it is so—it is a princely failing. And as long as this one roof shelters these good ladies—and I wish from my heart it may do so for many and many a long year to come—the tradition of genuine warm-hearted courteous Irish hospitality is still alive among us!

(*A hearty murmur of assent around the table*)

But we are living in a skeptical age and sometimes I fear that our new generations will lack these qualities of humanity, of hospitality, of kindly humour—which belonged to an older day. Listening a few moments ago to the names of these great singers of the past, it seemed to me, I must confess, that we are now living in a less—beautiful time.

BROWNE: Hear! Hear!

(*"Three Graces" instrumental begins to play and Gabriel steps back from the table. Though everyone else continues to watch "Gabriel" give his speech, Gabriel wanders around the table, watching the others watching and listening to "him." He speaks to us as the narrator*)

GABRIEL (*to the audience*): As I spoke that evening, I found my mind constantly wandering, drifting—first it was upon people who might be passing in the snow on the quay just outside. (*Looks out the "window"*) I imagined them gazing up at our lighted, beckoning window. Then drifted back upon all of us together, around this table. I found myself watching each face, each a map of life in flesh. Which chart

our days, our pains and joys, our losses, our loves.
Each face listening to the words I had so cautiously
collected and now—released.

BROWNE: Hear! Hear!

GABRIEL (*still to audience*): Second-hand, third-
hand, thoughts these were. Words so overused by
time as to have had their meanings beaten out of
them, much as an old sofa loses it stuffing. But no
one seemed to mind. Where are the words which
can express one's heart: I have not heard them.

(*Laughter at the table, the "speaker Gabriel" has told a
joke*)

So, they listened, as family and friends must and do,
with good humor and bright attention: those twin
threads that keep us together, keep us from split-
ting apart, keep us out of the dark that lies everywhere else. They watched. They listened. They
smiled. And if a mind drifted—(*He is now behind
Gretta, whose mind has drifted*) she tried to hide this
from the rest of us.

FREDDY: Hear! Hear!

(*Gabriel is back at the head of the table, instrumental
out, giving his speech*)

GABRIEL: Our paths through life are strewn with
many bad memories and were we to brood upon

them always we could not find the heart to go on bravely among the living.

OTHERS: Hear! Hear!

GABRIEL: Therefore, I will not linger on the past. I will not let any gloomy moralizing intrude upon us here tonight. Here we are gathered together for a brief moment from the bustle and rush of our everyday routine. We are met here as friends, in the spirit of good fellowship, as colleagues, as family, and as the guests of—what shall we call them?—the Three Graces of the Dublin Musical World!!

(*The table bursts into applause. "Three Graces" music starts*)

JULIA: I didn't hear . . .

MARY JANE: He said we are the Three Graces, Aunt Julia.

IVORS: The Three Graces.

(*Julia smiles and nods. Gabriel raises his glass and sings*):

GABRIEL:
I shall make a toast
A blessing on this house.
Timeless beauties each
And every one God's gift to us.

FREDDY: Timeless Beauties!

GABRIEL:
   Wherever we've wandered,
   Wherever we've roamed,
   We have known
   Your house to be our home.

   First there is Julia
   Her face a candle
   Lighting our way into the dark.

   Next is Aunt Kate.
   With a heart as large
   As a full moon over Dublin.

   And Mary Jane
   With Heaven's smile
   Sent to warm us on winter's night.

   Health and good cheer to
   Our Three Graces
   And every blessing be upon this house.

THE TABLE:
   Health and good cheer to
   Our Three Graces
   And every blessing be upon this house.

(*They drink, but Gabriel isn't finished yet. As he sings, Browne pours for himself. Freddy pours another for himself*)

GABRIEL:
   The world today
   Is thought-tormented.
   The world today
   Hyper-educated.
   The world today.
   The world today.

(*He raises his glass*)

   I shall make a toast
   A blessing on this house.
   Timeless beauties each
   And every one God's gift to us.

   Wherever we've wandered
   Wherever we've roamed
   We have known
   This house to be our home.

   God bless Julia
   With her pure laughter
   Easing the weight upon our souls.

   And bless our Aunt Kate
   With her loving tears
   Shed for all creatures of mankind.

   And bless Mary Jane
   With her lovely voice
   Like an angel's harp in the wind.

TABLE:
 Health and good cheer to
 Our Three Graces
 And every blessing be upon this house.

 Health and good cheer to
 Our Three Graces
 And every blessing be upon this house.

GABRIEL (*continuing*):
 Days gone by,
 Days lost,
 Days past,
 Days, let us call them,
 Spacious days.
 Days gone by.
 Days gone by.

GROUP:
 Health and good cheer to
 Our Three Graces
 And every blessing be upon this house.

 Always be merry our Three Graces
 And never lack for good company.

SECOND GROUP:
 Our Three Graces
 Our Three Graces
 Bless them each and every one.

THIRD GROUP
 Our Three Graces

**Our Three Graces
Bless them each and every one.**

GROUP:
　　**Always be merry our Three Graces
　　And never lack for good company.**

TABLE:
　　**Health and good cheer to
　　Our Three Graces
　　And every blessing be upon this house.**

(*All drink, sit. Gretta reaches over to touch Gabriel's hand*)

GRETTA:　That was lovely.

BROWNE:　Well done, Gabriel.

IVORS:　It was.

(*Silence. All are moved. Freddy suddenly starts whispering and tapping the table: "Speech! speech!"*)

GRETTA:　Julia, your turn.

(*And soon the others join in. All look to Julia. Julia then stands and there is silence. Julia looks to Kate, who is wiping her eyes, then to Mary Jane, who stands and heads for the piano*)

JULIA:　How can we respond to that? (*Beat*) Well, as has been our custom, my sister, my niece and I we have prepared something. Something perhaps more appropriate for the church organ at Adam and Eve's than our humble dining room. But, be that as it may, we are here and we do with what we have. (*Turns to Mary Jane*) Mary Jane?

(*Julia nods and Mary Jane plays. Julia and Kate look very somber—all expect a serious tune. After a short introduction, Julia begins "Naughty Girls"*)

JULIA (*sings*):
**I'm an imp on mischief bent
Only feeling quite content
When doing wrong.**

(*The table slowly begins to realize what she is singing. It is the last sort of song they expected to hear from Julia and she knows it. She winks at Kate and smiles*)

**At the Roman clubs, no doubt
Funny tales you hear about
My goings on.
Sometimes when I've had the fun
I repent on what I've done
But not for long
No, I break back into song.**

GRETTA (*laughing*): Oh, Aunt Julia!!!

JULIA:
**I'm a naughty girl
Naughty girl**

And Rome is in a whirl
Because I'm a naughty girl

FREDDY (*wagging his finger at her and laughing*):
Julia Morkan!!!

(*Everyone is laughing, enjoying this*)

JULIA:
I'm a naughty girl
Naughty girl
And Rome is in a whirl
'Cause I'm a naughty girl.

If I like to sit and chat
What can be the harm in that
Though the daylight's gone.
If I laugh a bit too loud
And that laughter draws a crowd,
Is it so very wrong.

If some youth with manners free
Dares to snatch a kiss from me,
Do we ask him to explain?
No!

JULIA, KATE AND MARY JANE:
We kiss him back again!
We are naughty girls
Naughty girls
And Rome is in a whirl
Because we're naughty girls.

We are naughty girls
Naughty girls.

KATE:
Because they're all afraid
Of this naughty little maid!

(*Mary Jane, Kate and Julia do a soft shoe for the incredulous guests*)

JULIA:
If some youth with manners free
Dares to snatch a kiss from me,
Do we ask him to explain?

EVERYONE: No!!!

JULIA, KATE AND MARY JANE:
We kiss him back again!
We are naughty girls
Naughty girls
And Rome is in a whirl
Because we're naughty girls

(*The three ladies start a snake-like chain around the table*)

We are naughty girls
Naughty girls
Because they're all afraid
Of this naughty little maid.

(*Freddy joins the ladies, then one by one the table gets up and joins the singing and dancing, soon holding hands*)

From left to right: Sally Ann Howes, Marni Nixon, Blair Brown and Christopher Walken in the 2000 Broadway production of James Joyce's The Dead. All photographs by Joan Marcus.

Left to right: Stephen Spinella, Alice Ripley, Emily Skinner and John Kelly in the 2000 Broadway production of James Joyce's The Dead.

Marni Nixon (left) and Sally Ann Howes in the 2000 Broadway production of James Joyce's the Dead.

The cast of the 2000 Broadway production of James Joyce's The Dead.

and making a long chain. The entire party—except for Lily, Michael and Rita, who come in and clean up the tables and chairs—begins to move around the room, then out the door and back, etc., singing)

ALL:
   They are naughty girls
   Naughty girls
   And Rome is in a whirl
   Because they're naughty girls.

   They are naughty girls
   Naughty girls
   Because they're all afraid
   Of this naughty little maid.

   They are naughty girls
   Naughty girls
   And Rome is in a whirl
   Because they're naughty girls.

   They are naughty girls
   Naughty girls
   Because they're all afraid
   Of this naughty little maid.

   They are naughty girls
   Naughty girls
   And Rome is in a whirl
   Because they're naughty girls.

   They are naughty girls
   Naughty girls

Because they're all afraid
Of this naughty little maid.

*(Julia suddenly breaks with the chain, holds her chest—
Gretta immediately sees this, grabs Gabriel and goes to
her and helps her sit. The others, though, don't notice
this as yet and continue to sing louder and louder)*

They are naughty girls
Naughty girls
And Rome is in a whirl
Because they're naughty girls

They are naughty girls
Naughty girls
Because they're all afraid
Of this naughty little maid

They are naughty girls
Naughty girls
And Rome is in a whirl
Because they're naughty girls

They are naughty girls . . .

*(Kate now sees Julia and leaves the line and goes to her.
The dancing continues louder still until there is a hard
banging—from Mr. Fulham below. Freddy is the last to
hear. And the song ends—interrupted—with others
telling Freddy to "Shsshh!!," the neighbors," "Mr. Fulham," etc. Freddy is furious and stomps on and yells at
the floor where the banging is coming from)*

FREDDY (*yelling at the floor*): Don't you shush us, Mr. Fulham!

(*Others try to shush Freddy. Gretta hurries to get water for Julia, others ask her how she is. A frustrated Freddy speaks to his mother, to drumbeat underscore*)

It's him. It's damn people like him who should leave us alone. It's him—him we should be shushing. What are we doing? What did we do wrong? Where's the harm in singing? Where's the harm in singing? You don't shush the singer, you listen to his song.

(*Music introduction*)

FREDDY (*sings*):
Now why can't we have a voice too
Why can't she have a voice or him or him?
How would he like it if we went

(*He stomps on the floor. Others try to stop him. More bangs from Mr. Fulham*)

It's him we have to shush whom I should
    have shushed
Him we have to shush all along.
It's him we have to shush to hear the singer
It's him we have to shush to hear the song.

You don't shush the singer, you let the singer
    sing
Who cares if you wake the neighbors.

(*Browne suddenly agrees and joins in*)

FREDDY AND BROWNE:
> You don't shush the singer you let the singer
> sing
> Who cares if we wake the dead.

(*Ivors joins*)

IVORS:
> So why can't we have a voice too
> Why can't he have a voice or him or him?

(*Lily and D'Arcy join*)

IVORS, D'ARCY AND LILY:
> How would they like it if we went

(*They stomp. Fulham bangs*)

FREDDY:
> It's him we have to shush whom we should
> have shushed
> Him we have to shush all along.
> It's him we have to shush to hear the singer.
> It's him we have to shush to hear the song.
>
> You don't shush the singer, you let the singer
> sing
> Who cares if we wake the neighbors.

FREDDY WITH OTHERS:
> You don't shush the singer you let the singer
> sing
> Who cares if we wake the dead.

ALL (*except the Three Graces, to Mr. Fulham*):
  Health and good cheer
  To our Three Graces
  And every blessing be upon this house!!!

JULIA (*standing*): Dance!!

FREDDY (*to everyone*): Dance!!

(*All clear the furniture to the sides, including the carpet, as Freddy gets the dancing started*)

FREDDY:
  So what if we do wake the neighbors up
  So what if our revelry wakes the dead?

FREDDY AND GRETTA:
  So what if we do wake the neighbors up
  So what if our revelry wakes the dead?

FREDDY:
  You don't shush the singer
  You let the singer sing
  Who cares if we wake neighbors.

ALL:
  You don't shush the singer
  You let the singer sing
  Who cares if we wake the dead?

FREDDY:
  They've been asleep since God knows when
  And they'll soon be sound asleep again.

ALL:
　They've been asleep since God knows when
　And they'll soon be sound asleep again.

FREDDY:
　You don't shush the singer
　You let the singer sing
　Who cares if we wake neighbors.

ALL:
　You don't shush the singer
　You let the singer sing
　Who cares if we wake the dead?

FREDDY:
　You don't shush the singer
　You let the singer sing
　Who cares if we wake neighbors.

ALL:
　You don't shush the singer
　You let the singer sing
　Who cares if we wake the dead!

MICHAEL:　Highland fling!

(*Dance break. Young ones dance and the others cheer them on as their feet pound on the floor, keeping Mr. Fulham awake*)

ALL:
　Wake the dead
　They've slept long enough

And they'll soon be asleep again
Wake the dead

IVORS: How's that, Mr. Fulham!

ALL:
They've slept long enough
And they'll soon be asleep again.
Wake the dead
They've slept long enough
And they'll soon be asleep again
Wake the dead
They've slept long enough
And they'll soon be asleep again.
Wake the dead
They've slept long enough
And they'll soon be asleep again
Wake the dead
They've slept long enough
And they'll soon be asleep again.
Wake the dead
They've slept long enough
And they'll soon be asleep again
Wake the dead
They've slept long enough
And they'll soon be asleep again.
Wake the dead
They've slept long enough
And they'll soon be asleep again
Wake the dead
They've slept long enough
And they'll soon be asleep again.
Wake the dead!!

Scene Three

Gabriel speaks to the audience and as he does so, the setting is changed from the dining room to Aunt Julia's bedroom. As Gabriel speaks he watches this transformation.

GABRIEL: With the dead now awake, Mary Jane was entreated to play her academy piece—full of runs and difficult passages.

(He listens for a moment as Mary Jane plays the piano)

The only person who seemed to follow the music was Mary Jane herself, her hands racing along the keyboard or lifted from it at the pauses *(Mary Jane and those watching her, freeze, then exit. Music out)*—like those of a priestess in a moment of high curse. Aunt Julia had retreated here, to the sanctum sanctorum. Her bedroom, where the Pope himself would have felt it safe to store his greatest treasures, of which Aunt Julia surely must be one.

(Aunt Julia has entered. She goes to the bed and sits)

A picture of the balcony scene from *Romeo and Juliet* hung on that wall. And beside it, another of the two murdered princes in the tower which Aunt Julia herself had worked in red, blue and brown wools when she was a girl. Probably in the school they had gone to as girls that kind of work had been taught. *(Remembering)* Certainly my mother learned it. For one birthday she worked for me a waistcoat of purple tabinet with little foxes' heads upon it, lined with brown satin and having round mulberry buttons. (*Gabriel takes a photo off the piano*) Her photograph. My mother. (*He shows us*) She holds an open book upon her knee. That is Constantine, my brother, at her feet. He's dressed in his man-o-war suit. (*Gabriel looks at the photo, then places it on the table in Julia's bedroom*) Gretta nursed her during her last long illness in our house. Gretta—who once she had called "country cute." (*Piano starts offstage*) In the drawing room, Mary Jane ended with a trill of octaves in the treble and a final deep octave in the bass. I led the applause.

(*Applause, then low chatter and music offstage. Gabriel applauds and exits off to the drawing room. Kate has entered the bedroom*)

KATE (*holding a hot water bottle*): Such a lovely party, hasn't it been? And that speech by Gabriel. He sounds more and more like his grandfather every day. Put this under you.

(*Kate tries to hand Julia the hot water bottle*)

JULIA: I'm not cold.

KATE: Do as I say.

JULIA: I won't.

KATE: You are the most stubborn woman I know.

JULIA: Am I?

KATE: You won't do anything I say, why?

JULIA: Sh-sh . . .

KATE: Take the bottle!

JULIA: No!

(*Mary Jane and Gabriel enter*)

MARY JANE (*entering*): I don't deserve a bit of the credit, Gabriel. They have done the work. And haven't they done a grand job? A niece couldn't be blessed with two finer aunts.

GABRIEL: She couldn't. And nor could a nephew.

MARY JANE: And such young souls, too! Sometimes I confess to feeling like I'm the oldest in the house!

JULIA: Are they leaving?

GABRIEL: Very soon, Aunt Julia. How are you feeling?

(*Kate is on the verge of tears*)

MARY JANE: Browne is out there, Aunt Kate.

KATE: Browne is everywhere. Really, he is very attentive.

JULIA: He's been installed here like the gas all during Christmas. (*The sisters laugh—a cough from Browne*) Tell him to come in, Mary Jane. (*Browne coughs in the hallway. Mary Jane goes to get him*) I hope to goodness he didn't hear me.

GABRIEL (*to Julia picking up hot water bottle*): Perhaps you'd care for this.

JULIA: Oh how thoughtful. I am feeling chilled.

(*Kate is hurt. Mary Jane enters with Browne*)

BROWNE: The inner sanctum! The lady's chamber! How glorious you look there, my lady.

JULIA: Now don't come too close. I can imagine what you smell like.

BROWNE (*to Kate*): Is she going to be alright?

KATE: She'll be fine. (*Trying not to cry*) I must go see how Lily is getting on. Excuse me (*Kate hurries out*)

JULIA: She's getting old. She cries like that all the time. It gets tiring, if the truth be told.

BROWNE: The Misses Morkan! Dublin's—naughty girls! If I had only known, I could have been booking you for years!

JULIA: I said to Kate—when choosing which song to sing—I said this year, haven't we heard enough of the Church's music? After all, hasn't the Church heard enough of me?

MARY JANE: Why'd you say that? Aunt Julia you know that's not true.

JULIA (*over this, to Browne*): You're leaving?

BROWNE: Soon. It was a glorious evening.

JULIA: I don't envy you your journey home at this hour.

BROWNE: I'd like nothing better this minute than a rattling fine walk in the country or a fast drive with a good spanking goer between the shafts.

JULIA: We used to have a very good horse and trap at home.

MARY JANE: The never-to-be-forgotten Johnny.

JULIA: You remember.

BROWNE: Well now, what was so wonderful about Johnny?

(*Music can be heard from the drawing room*)

JULIA: The late lamented Patrick Morkan—their grandfather, he was a glue-boiler.

GABRIEL: He had a starch mill.

JULIA: He had a horse by the name of Johnny. And Johnny used to work in the mill, walking round and round in order to drive the mill. Which was all very well, but now comes the tragic part. One fine day the old gentleman thought he'd like to drive out to the park.

MARY JANE: Lord have mercy on his soul.

JULIA: Amen. As I said, so the old gentleman harnessed Johnny, put on his very best tall hat and very best stock collar and drove out in grand style.

GABRIEL: This was in Back Lane.

JULIA: Oh, Gabriel, he didn't live in Back Lane. Only the mill was there. So out he drove with Johnny. And everything went beautifully until Johnny comes in sight of King Billy's statue—now whether he falls in love with the horse King Billy sits on or whether he thought he was back again in the mill, anyhow he began to walk round and round the statue! (*Laughing*) With the old gentleman pompous-like shouting—

(*Julia starts coughing. Everyone quiets down. Offstage music stops. Slowly, Julia gets her breath back*)

MARY JANE: It is the weather.

GABRIEL: Everybody has colds.

MARY JANE: They say we haven't had snow like this

71

for thirty years. I read in the newspaper that the snow is to be general all over Ireland.

JULIA: I love the snow. (*Beat. Referring to the offstage music and chatter*) They've stopped.

MARY JANE: It's late.

JULIA: What is it about snow? That feels so—forgiving?

(*Kate bursts in*)

KATE: Julia, cover your eyes! Everyone cover your eyes! Are they covered?

(*Kate hurries off and immediately returns with D'Arcy in tow. He looks around. Gretta, Miss Ivors and Malins follow on to watch. D'Arcy then begins to sing to Julia— beautifully—an aria in Italian. As he begins, Julia uncovers her eyes to watch*)

D'ARCY (*sings*):
Se tu sei veramente la ragazza
Come pretendi di essere
Menzione la prima promessa
Che ci scambiammo
Oh non ti ricordi.

La notte della nostra prima volta
Su quella collina fredda
Quando il incontrammo
Il cui racconto adesso mi da pene.

Casca la pioggia
Sulle mie ciocche
E la rugiada
Bagna la mia pelle
Il mio bambino freddo
Fra le mie braccie
Signore mi faccie entrare
Signore mi faccie entrare.

(*Gasps. They are much affected by the singing. Pause*)

IVORS: I have been at him all evening. He said he had a dreadful cold and couldn't sing.

KATE: Oh, Mr. D'Arcy now that was a great fib to tell.

D'ARCY: Can't you see that I'm as hoarse as a crow?

JULIA: It's the weather. Gabriel was saying everyone had colds.

D'ARCY: A lovely song, is it not?

MARY JANE: Very nice.

MRS. MALINS: I'm just sorry Mr. D'Arcy wasn't in voice tonight.

KATE (*at the same time*): Now, Mrs. Malins, don't annoy Mr. D'Arcy. I won't have him annoyed.

GRETTA: Mr. D'Arcy where's it from? I don't think I've heard anything so—lovely?

D'ARCY: It is from the third act of *Le Droghe D'Amore*. Do you know the opera? (*He looks around the room*) Pity. It's a beautiful but neglected work. It's title means—

GABRIEL: The Drug of Love.

D'ARCY: Correct. The Drug of Love. Should any of you ever have the opportunity . . . I would not miss it.

MARY JANE: And what is its story, Mr. D'Arcy?

D'ARCY: Unrequited love.

JULIA: And the woman? Does she die?

D'ARCY: In the final act. And most—beautifully.

(*Freddy and Michael burst in, conspiratorially looking for Gabriel, Browne and D'Arcy*)

JULIA: Now what is happening?

BROWNE (*to Julia, gently*): Sh-sh. Sh-sh.

GRETTA (*explaining to Julia*): The boys have been practicing, Aunt Julia.

(*The men group themselves as they have rehearsed in the drawing room and now sing to Julia*)

THE FIVE MEN:
Goodnight, sleep tight

You queen of our hearts
Cuddle in your bed tonight.
Goodnight, goodnight.

Sweet dreams, sweet dreams
You queen of our hearts
As with fairy dust
We leave our love for you.

Our Three Graces, Our Three Graces
Bless this very special one.

Your pillow he's a lucky fellow
His hand upon your head
All alone with you in bed.
May your dreams be always dreamy
May your sleep be always sleepy
May your toes be warmed for evermore.

Goodnight, sleep tight
You queen of our hearts
Cuddle in your bed tonight.
Goodnight, goodnight.

Sweet dreams, sweet dreams
You queen of our hearts
As with fairy dust
We leave our love for you.

Your pillow he's a lucky fellow
His hand upon your head
All alone with you in bed.
May your dreams be always dreamy

May your sleep be always sleepy
May you slumber, may you snooze
The night away and never lose
Your zest for rising up tomorrow morning
As the sun comes up
May your toes be warmed for evermore.

Goodnight.

(*Julia has fallen asleep. Silence. Whispers amongst themselves*)

IVORS: I should go.

GRETTA (*to Ivors*): But Molly, how can you get home?

IVORS: Oh, it's only two steps up the quay.

GABRIEL: If you will allow us, Miss Ivors, we'll see you home.

IVORS: I won't hear of it. I'm quite well able to take care of myself. (*Beat*) And besides, Michael has already offered.

(*All begin to leave. Miss Ivors slips her arm around Michael's. Quiet good-byes from everyone*)

LILY: I could only get the one cab, so far.

GABRIEL: We'll find another along the quay. Freddy, you take it. Your mother should not be standing out in the snow.

FREDDY: Oh thank you, Gabriel.

BROWNE: I'll take a ride with you, Teddy.

FREDDY: Why do you call me Teddy? You know my name. We're friends.

BROWNE: I don't know why I do it. I just do.

(*One by one they leave. Gabriel and Gretta are left alone with the sleeping Julia. Offstage more good-byes and a door slam, which wakes up Julia*)

GABRIEL: There's no—draft?

JULIA: No. Go. It's over. And thank you both for everything. (*Offstage we hear the others singing "Naughty Girls"*) And especially for that wonderful speech, Gabriel.

(*He hugs her*)

GRETTA: Goodnight, Aunt Julia. (*She hugs Julia*)

JULIA: And now I suppose you must go all the way home to Monkstown. I'm sorry.

GRETTA: No, we're staying the night at the Gresham, Aunt Julia.

JULIA: That's a splendid idea. The children will enjoy that.

GRETTA: The children are at home, Aunt Julia.

JULIA: Listen, they're singing again. (*Listens*) I'll be apologizing to the neighbors for weeks.

GRETTA: Well, goodnight then.

GABRIEL: Goodnight, Aunt Julia. (*Gabriel and Gretta start to exit then he comes back*) I'll come by on Saturday.

(*Gabriel and Gretta exit and offstage door slams. Silence. Song continues from outside. Julia tries not to cry, when suddenly a young girl in a nightgown appears and sits on Julia's bed*)

JULIA (*startled*): Oh, who are you? (*Beat*) Me? I was talking about you just tonight. Now what was I saying? I was telling them when I was young, my voice wasn't too bad was it? When I was young, some people thought it quite a lovely voice. It was lovely wasn't it?

YOUNG JULIA (*sings*):
When lovely lady stoops to folly
And finds too late that men betray
What charms can soothe her melancholy
What art can wash her grief away?

JULIA: Yes, yes—that is exactly how I used to sing it. Not so sad. (*Sings*)
The only art her guilt to cover
To hide her shame from every eye,
To give repentance to her lover,
And wring his bosom, is—to die

(*Kate re-enters, quickly crossing to bedside table for a coin purse. She cannot see the Young Julia*)

KATE: Freddy doesn't have a coin with him.

(*Gabriel enters as narrator—watching*)

JULIA: And the musicians? Have they been taken care of?

KATE: Lily's handing them their pies now. (*Kate exits quickly with the purse*)

GABRIEL (*to audience*): She slept peacefully that night. And the next. And a third. And, as promised, I returned on Saturday, but dressed now in black, with a band about my arm, seeking words to express our loss . . . and finding none.

BOTH JULIAS (*sing*):
When lovely lady stoops to folly
And finds too late that men betray
What charms can soothe her melancholy,
What art can wash her grief away?

(*Lights fade on all but Gabriel*)

Scene Four

The Gresham. "Michael Furey" instrumental.

GABRIEL (*to audience*): In our room that night at the Gresham, I watched my wife undress. (*Gretta enters and sits. She is now in her night clothes*) So frail she seemed, so light, so erect. I longed to defend her against—something.

(*Beat*)

Years of memories rush as I watch: A heliotrope envelope lying beside my breakfast cup. From her. I hold it. I caress it. Birds outside twittering in the ivy. The sunny web of the curtain shimmers across the floor. I could not eat that morning—for happiness.

(*Beat*)

Another: a crowded platform. I place the ticket inside of the warm soft, slightly moist—palm of her glove.

(*Beat*)

Yet another—outside, looking in, through a grated window at a man making bottles in a roaring furnace. It is very cold outside. Her face, that face, fragrant in the cold air, is close to mine. And she suddenly shouts to the man at the furnace: "Is the fire hot, sir?"

(*Beat*)

> I could hear the falling of the candle's molten wax into the tray and the thumping of my own heart.

(*Beat*)

> She said to the porter that she didn't want any light. That there was light enough from the street. It could have been our honeymoon . . .

(*Beat*)

> But it wasn't.

(*Lights up at the Gresham Hotel room. "Michael Furey" instrumental ends*)

GABRIEL (*to Gretta*): You look tired.

GRETTA: I suppose I am a little.

(*Gretta heads towards the bed, he tries to stop her, but she hardly responds*)

GABRIEL: You don't feel ill now?

GRETTA: Ill? No, tired, that's all.

GABRIEL: By the way . . . you know Freddy Malins?

GRETTA: Yes, what about him?

GABRIEL: Well, poor fellow—he's a decent sort of chap after all. He gave me back the sovereign I lent him and I didn't expect it, really. (*Beat*) It's a pity he couldn't keep away from that Browne, because he's not a bad fellow at heart.

(*Short pause*)

GRETTA: When did you lend him the sovereign?

GABRIEL: Oh, before Christmas. When he opened that little Christmas card shop on Henry Street.

GRETTA: You are a very generous person, Gabriel Conroy.

GABRIEL: What's wrong?

GRETTA: Why does something have to be—?

GABRIEL: What is the matter Gretta? You are not yourself. Have I done something to—

GRETTA: You? No. No. You've done nothing.

GABRIEL: You've been crying.

GRETTA: Oh, I am just thinking about that silly song. "Lean out of the window, Goldenhair . . ." (*Gabriel looks at her, confused*) That boy, one of Mary Jane's pupils? Michael? He reminded me of someone. It took me the longest time to figure out who . . . (*Beat*) A someone who used to sing that song.

GABRIEL: And that makes you cry? That makes no sense. Who was this "someone"?

GRETTA: Gabriel, it was long ago. I'd forgotten—

GABRIEL: Who was this someone long ago?

GRETTA: I was a girl. I have children of my own now. I have you—

GABRIEL: Gretta, tell me!

GRETTA: It was a person I used to know in Galway when I was living with my grandmother.

GABRIEL: Someone you were in love with?

GRETTA: It was a boy I used to know. Named Michael, too. Michael—Furey. He used to sing that song. Suddenly I could see him so plainly—

GABRIEL: You were in love with him.

GRETTA: Please don't get upset—

GABRIEL: Perhaps that was why you wanted to go to Galway with Molly Ivors.

GRETTA: Why would I—?

GABRIEL: To see him perhaps?

GRETTA: No.

GABRIEL: Is that why?

GRETTA: No.

GABRIEL: Gretta, is that why?

GRETTA: No. You don't understand. No!

GABRIEL: Does he write you?!

GRETTA: No.

GABRIEL: Do you write him!!

GRETTA: No! No! No!

(*"Michael Furey" intro begins*)

GABRIEL: Gretta, I'm sorry. I am sorry. You are right. I don't understand. But I'm sure if it was so important, you'd have told me about this Michael Furey before. Isn't that so? (*Suddenly, with a shock, he realizes the depth, the seriousness of this*) Gretta . . .

(*She tries to wipe her tears. Now she has to explain*)

GRETTA: Michael Furey—Michael Furey—Michael Furey—he was very delicate. Such eyes he had, big dark eyes. I used to walk with him . . . he died. (*Sings*)

Isn't it a terrible thing
To die so young
He was only seventeen

It was in the winter
And I was leaving Galway
Leaving him so poorly
O, Michael.

Michael Furey
He was very fond of me
Such eyes he had
Big dark eyes
I used to walk with him
With him.

When the time came to go
I wrote to him
Saying I'd be back again
In the summer.
That night I heard stones
On my window.
I ran downstairs into the garden
Where Michael stood by the wall.

I can see his eyes
As he shivered in the rain
I implored him to go home again
That he would catch his death,
But he said
I do not wish to live
And when I was only a week up here
I heard Michael Furey was dead.

Michael Furey
He was very delicate
Such eyes he had

Big dark eyes
I think he died for me
For me.

(*Gabriel tries for a moment to grasp what she has just told him. This woman who he thought he knew better than himself has revealed a whole other world inside her. Here is the crack, the unimaginable depth he spoke to us about early in the play*)

GABRIEL: For you. (*Beat*) This boy died for you? (*Gretta looks at him, she begins to sob*) So it was him you were thinking about when you sang—

GRETTA: Gabriel—

GABRIEL: I just want to know if it was him—

GRETTA: Gabriel.

GABRIEL: And I suppose you loved him too? (*Beat*) Loved him more than—anything?

(*He stands and speaks to the audience*)

And so the world is like the surface of a frozen lake, we walk along, we slip, we try to keep our balance and not to fall, but then one day there's a crack— and so we learn that underneath us is an unimagined depth just below.

(*Beat*)

For perhaps an hour, maybe two—time has no meaning here—I watched the falling of the snow outside our window. And listened to the weeping of my wife.

GRETTA: I'm sorry Gabriel, I'm sorry. (*She cries*)

(*He turns and watches the snow fall outside the bedroom window. As he watches, he begins to sing to himself*)

GABRIEL (*singing*):
Snow will be general
All over Ireland
Falling on every part
Of the dark central plain.
Falling softly upon the Bog of Allen
And, further westward,
Into the dark mutinous Shannon waves.

Softly falling through the universe
Softly falling upon our bed
Upon your white back
Upon your red hair,
Upon all the living and the dead.

Snow will be general
All over Ireland
Falling on the churchyard
Where lies Michael Furey's grave.
Lying thickly upon the crooked crosses
And on the headstones,
On the spears of the gate,
On the barren stones.

Softly falling through the universe
Softly falling upon our bed.
Upon Aunt Julia
So near to death today
Upon all the living and the dead.

Snow will be falling
All over Ireland
Faintly falling
Upon our loved ones
Upon our country
Upon our souls.

(*The company enters and sings to him*)

GABRIEL AND COMPANY:
Snow will be falling
Falling softly,
Faintly falling
All over Ireland
Snow will be falling
Snow will be falling
Snow will be falling
Upon the living and the dead.

GABRIEL:
Upon the living and the dead.

(*Gabriel looks at his wife. She turns to him, and holds him*)